100 facts
EXPLORING SPACE

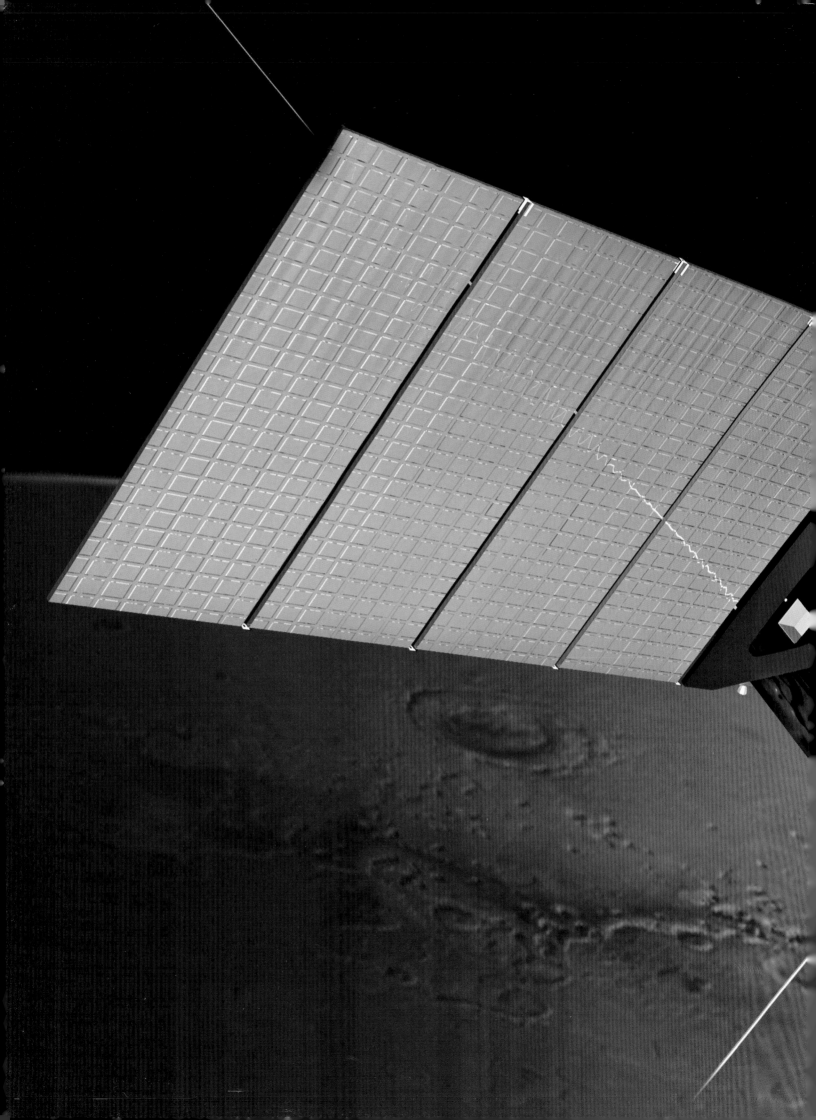

100 facts

EXPLORING SPACE

Steve Parker
Consultant: Clint Twist

Miles
KeLLY

First published in 2011 by Miles Kelly Publishing Ltd
Harding's Barn, Bardfield End Green, Thaxted, Essex, CM6 3PX, UK

This edition printed in 2011

2 4 6 8 10 9 7 5 3

PUBLISHING DIRECTOR Belinda Gallagher
CREATIVE DIRECTOR Jo Cowan
EDITOR Carly Blake
VOLUME DESIGNERS Jo Cowan, Andrea Slane
IMAGE MANAGER Liberty Newton
INDEXER Eleanor Holme
PRODUCTION MANAGER Elizabeth Collins
REPROGRAPHICS Stephan Davis, Jennifer Hunt
ASSETS Lorraine King

ISBN 978-1-84810-473-0

Printed in China

British Library Cataloguing-in-Publication Data
A catalogue record for this book is available from the British Library

ACKNOWLEDGEMENTS
The publishers would like to thank the following artists who have contributed to this book:
Julian Baker, Mike Foster (Maltings Partnership), Alex Pang, Rocket Design, Mike Saunders
All other artwork from the Miles Kelly Artwork Bank

The publishers would like to thank the following sources for the use of their photographs:
t = top, b = bottom, l = left, r = right, c = centre, bg = background
Cover: front NASA/JPL/Cornell University/Maas Digital;
back(t) NASA, (cl) NASA/Goddard Space Flight Center Scientific Visualization Studio, (cr) NASA

Alamy 29(tr) Keith Morris **Corbis** 15 Roger Ressmeye; 25(t) Michael Benson/Kinetikon Pictures; 34(t) Bill Ingalls/NASA/
Handout/CNP; 35(t) Roger Ressmeyer **European Space Agency (ESA)** 2–3 Alex Lutkus; 18(r) D. Ducros; 33 *Mars Express* D. Ducros;
34–35(b); 37(bl) 2007 MPS/DLR-PF/IDA; 43(tl) ESA/NASA/JPL/University of Arizona; 45(t) C. Carreau, (tr) AOES Medialab
Fotolia.com 8(bl) D.aniel **Getty** 31(br) Time & Life Pictures; 30–31(bg) SSPL via Getty Images; 42 Time & Life Pictures
iStockphoto.com 14–15(bg) Nicholas Belton; 22(r) Jan Rysavy **NASA** 5(main), (tl) JPL; 9(b) JPL-Caltech; 13(bl); 14(c) JPL-Caltech,
(t) NASA Langley Research Center (NASA-LaRC); 14–15(b); 18(bl); 18–19(t) Johns Hopkins University Applied Physics
Laboratory/Southwest Research Institute; 20(c) JPL/University of Arizona; 20–21 oval insets JPL; 22(c); 23 Saturn JPL, Comet Borrelly
JPL, Uranus, Neptune, *Voyager 2* gold disk, *Deep Space 1*; 24(bl) STEREO; 25; 27(bl), (br); 30(bl) JPL/Cornell; 32–33(bg) JPL/Cornell;
32(bl) Goddard Space Flight Center Scientific Visualization Studio, *Mariner 4* JPL, *Mariner 9* JPL, *Mars 3* Russian Space Research Institute
(IKI), Viking lander, *Mars Global Surveyor*; 33 *Sojourner* JPL-Caltech, *Spirit/Opportunity* rover JPL, *Mars Reconnaissance Orbiter* JPL; 34–35(bg);
39(br); 41(c), (b); 44(bl) Johns Hopkins University Applied Physics Laboratory/Southwest Research Institute; 45(br); 46–47(bg) JPL-
Caltech/T. Pyle (SSC) **Rex Features** 27(tl); 35(br) NASA; 46(tl) Everett Collection, (c) c.Paramount/Everett; 47(b) KeystoneUSA-ZUMA
Reuters 9(t) Kimimasa Mayama **Science Photo Library** 6–7 European Space Agency; 11(b) NASA; 16–17 David Ducros; 19(r) David
Parker; 27(tr) NASA; 28 Detlev Van Ravenswaay; 30–31(c); 33(tr) NASA/JPL/UA/Lockheed Martin, (b) NASA/JPL-Caltech,
(tl) NASA/JPL/UA/Lockheed Martin; 36(t) SOHO/ESA/NASA; 37(tl) NASA; 38 Chris Butler; 41(t) NASA/JPL
Shutterstock.com 8–9(c) pio3; 10–11(bg) Phase4Photography; 12–13(bg) SURABKY; 19(l) jamie cross; 18–19(bg) plavusa87;
22–23(bg) plavusa87

All other photographs are from:
PhotoDisc, Flat Earth

Every effort has been made to acknowledge the source and copyright holder of each picture.
Miles Kelly Publishing apologises for any unintentional errors or omissions.

Made with paper from a sustainable forest

www.mileskelly.net info@mileskelly.net

www.factsforprojects.com

CONTENTS

To boldly go...

1 **For thousands of years people gazed up at the night sky and wondered what it would be like to explore space.** This became a reality around 50 years ago, and since then humans have been to the Moon, and unmanned spacecraft have visited all of the planets in the Solar System. Spacecraft have also explored other planets' moons, asteroids and glowing comets. These amazing discoveries help us to understand the Universe.

▶ ESA's *Integral* satellite (launched in 2002) is deployed from a Proton rocket to observe invisible gamma rays in space. Since 1957, humans have sent spacecraft to all eight planets in the Solar System, as well as more than 50 moons, asteroids and comets.

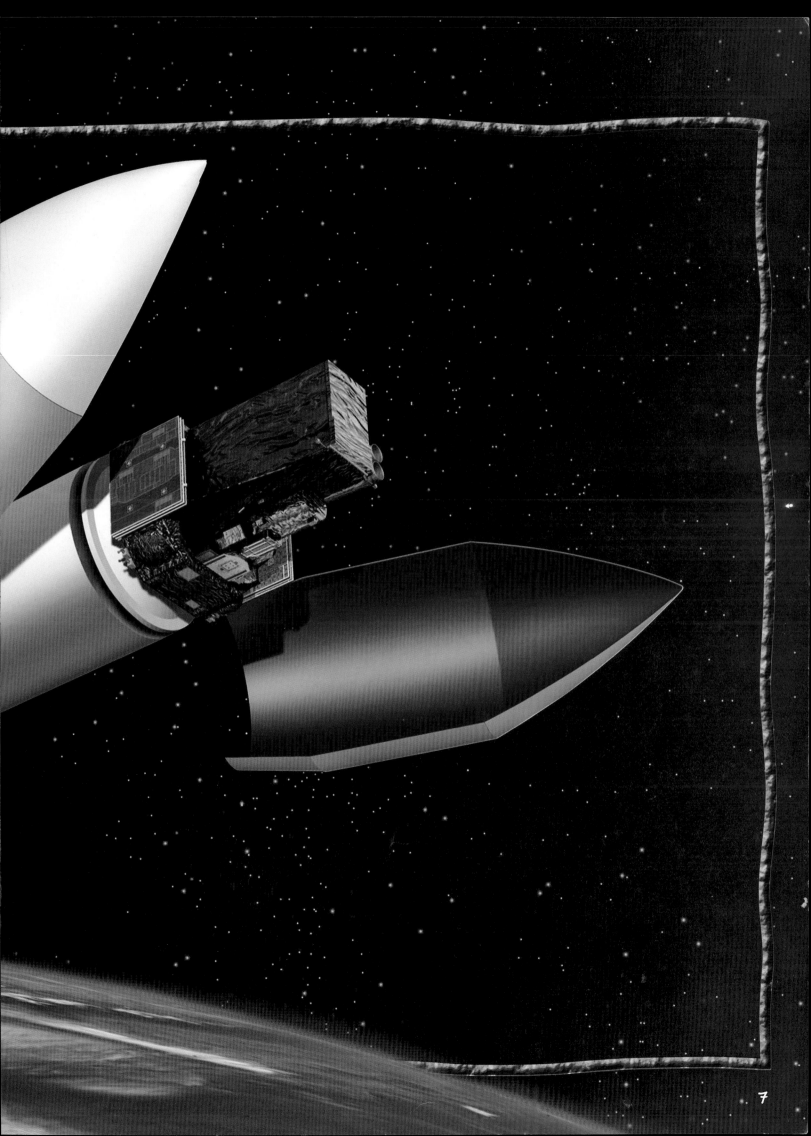

Who explores, and why?

2 Exploring space involves sending craft, robots, equipment and sometimes people to planets, moons, asteroids and comets. Some craft fly near to their targets, while others land. As they explore, they gather information to send back to Earth.

3 Space exploration is different from other space sciences. For example, astronomy is the study of objects in space including planets, stars and galaxies, as well as the Universe as a whole. Much of this is done using telescopes, rather than travelling out into space.

天文學
銀河

Vandenberg Air Force Base and Spaceport, California, USA

NORTH AMERICA

NASA Headquarters, Washington D.C., USA

Kennedy Space Center, Florida, USA

Alcantara Launch Center, Sao Luis, Brazil

Guiana Space Centre, Kourou, French Guiana

SOUTH AMERICA

▼ Astronomers use huge, extremely powerful telescopes to observe outer space from Earth.

▲ Space mission headquarters and launch sites are spread across the world.

4 Space exploration is complicated and expensive. Generally, only large nations, such as the USA, Russia, Japan and Europe, send craft into space. Recently, China and India have also launched exploratory missions.

5 Sending even a small spacecraft into space costs vast amounts of money. The Japanese *Hayabusa* mission to bring back samples of the comet Itokawa began in 2003. It lasted seven years and cost around $170 million. Sending the *Phoenix* lander to Mars in 2008 was even more expensive, at $450 million dollars.

▶ The comet-visiting *Hayabusa* spacecraft blasted off from Uchinoura Space Centre, Japan, in 2003. It returned to Earth in 2010, carrying samples of comet dust.

European Space Agency Headquarters, Paris, France

Roscomos Headquarters, Moscow, Russia

ASIA

EUROPE

Uchinoura Space Centre, Japan

Xichang Satellite Launch Center, China

Balkonur Cosmodrome (Russian), Kazakhstan

AFRICA

Tanegashima Space Center, Japan

Shar Space Launch Center, Sriharikota Island, India

▼ Recent observations in space suggest faraway stars could have planets forming around them from bits of gas, dust and rock — similiar to our own Solar System.

6 If the costs are so great, why do we explore space? Exploring the unknown has long been a part of human nature. Space exploration provides clues that may help us to understand how the Universe formed. Progress in space technology can also help advances on Earth.

Early explorers

7 The Space Age began in 1957 when Russia launched *Sputnik 1*, the first Earth-orbiting satellite. It was a metal, ball-shaped craft that could measure pressure and temperature, and send radio signals back to Earth.

▼ Tracking *Sputnik 1*'s orbit showed how the upper atmosphere of the Earth fades into space.

8 In 1958, the USA launched the satellite *Explorer 1*. As it orbited the Earth it detected two doughnut-shaped belts of high-energy particles, known as the Van Allen Belts. They can damage spacecraft and interfere with radio signals.

◀ The Van Allen belts are made up of particles, trapped by Earth's natural magnetic field.

Inner belt

Outer belt

Heat-resistant outer casing

Inner casing

9 In 1959, Russia's *Luna 1* spacecraft was aiming for the Moon, but it missed. Later that year, *Luna 2* crashed into the Moon on purpose, becoming the first craft to reach another world. On its way down the craft measured the Moon's gravity and magnetism.

Batteries

Antennae

Ventilation fan

QUIZ
Early exploration was a 'Space Race' between the USA and the Soviet Union. Which had these 'firsts'?
1. First satellite in space
2. First person in space
3. First craft on the Moon
4. First person on the Moon

Answers:
1, 2, 3 – Russia 4 – USA

Hatch

Heat shield
covering

Long range
antenna

◀ Gagarin's *Vostok 1*
spacecraft was ten
times larger than the
Sputnik 1 satellite,
and 50 times
heavier.

Descent module –
only this ball-shaped
part came back
to Earth

Oxygen and nitrogen
gas tanks for fuel and
for Gagarin to breathe

Retro-thruster

10 **The first person in space was Russian
cosmonaut Yuri Gagarin.** In 1961 he made one
orbit of Earth in the spacecraft *Vostok 1*. The
furthest he travelled into space was 327 kilometres.
Gagarin's trip made news around the world and
showed that humans could survive in space.

11 **The US sent seven
Surveyor craft to the Moon
between 1966 and 1968.** Five
succeeded in soft-landing (landing
without being destroyed) on the surface.
This was an important stage in planning
the most exciting and ambitious mission
of all – sending people to another world.

▶ *Surveyor 3* landed on the Moon in
April 1967. It was photographed by the
Apollo 12 astronauts in November 1969.

Man on the Moon!

12 The only humans to have explored another world are 12 US astronauts that were part of the Apollo program. Six Apollo missions landed on the Moon between 1969 and 1972, each with two astronauts. First to step onto the surface were Neil Armstrong and Buzz Aldrin from *Apollo 11*, on 20 July, 1969.

13 Each Apollo lunar lander touched down on a different type of terrain. The astronauts stayed on the Moon for three or four days. They explored, carried out experiments and collected samples of Moon dust and rocks to bring back to Earth.

14 The last three Apollo missions took a Lunar Roving Vehicle (LRV), or 'Moon buggy'. The astronauts drove for up to 20 kilometres at a time, exploring the Moon's hills, valleys, flat plains and cliffs.

15 Since the Apollo missions, more than 50 unmanned spacecraft have orbited or landed on the Moon. In 1994, US orbiter *Clementine* took many photographs, gravity readings and detailed maps of the Moon's surface.

◀ *Apollo 15*'s Lunar Module pilot James Irwin salutes the US flag and his Commander David Scott, in 1971. Their Lunar Module lander is behind and the Moon buggy is to the right.

MISSION	DATE	CREW	ACHIEVEMENT
Apollo 11	July 1969	Neil Armstrong (C) Buzz Aldrin (LMP) Michael Collins (CMP)	First humans on another world
Apollo 12	November 1969	Pete Conrad (C) Alan Bean (LMP) Richard Gordon (CMP)	First colour television pictures of the Moon returned to Earth
Apollo 13	April 1970	James Lovell (C) Fred Haise (LMP) Ken Mattingly (CMP)	Apollo 13 turned back after launch because of an explosion. It never reached the Moon, but returned safely to Earth
Apollo 14	January–February 1971	Alan Shepard (C) Edgar Mitchell (LMP) Stuart Roosa (CMP)	Longest Moon walks in much improved spacesuits
Apollo 15	July–August 1971	David Scott (C) James Irwin (LMP) Alfred Worden (CMP)	First use of a Moon buggy allowed astronauts to explore a wider range
Apollo 16	April 1972	John Young (C) Charles Duke (LMP) Thomas Mattingly (CMP)	First and only mission to land in the Moon's highlands
Apollo 17	December 1972	Eugene Cernan (C) Harrison Schmitt (LMP) Ronald Evans (CMP)	Returned a record 49 kilograms of rock and dust samples

16 In 2009, the *Lunar Reconnaissance Orbiter* began mapping the Moon's surface in detail. Its pictures showed parts of the Apollo craft left by the astronauts. In the same year the Indian orbiter *Chandrayaan 1* discovered ice on the Moon.

◀ On each mission, the Commander (C) and the Lunar Module pilot (LMP) landed on the Moon, while the Command Module pilot (CMP) stayed in the orbiting craft.

Plan and prepare

17 Planning a mission takes many years. Scientists suggest places to explore, what might be discovered, and the cost. Their government must agree for the mission to go ahead.

▲ In 1961 US space engineer John Houbolt developed the idea of using a three-part spacecraft for the Apollo Moon missions.

18 There are many types of exploratory missions. A flyby takes the spacecraft near to its target world, and past. An orbiter circles around the target. A lander mission touches down on the surface. A lander may release a rover, which can travel around on the surface.

▲ For worlds with an atmosphere, parachutes are used to lower a lander gently. This parachute design for a planned mission to Mars is being tested in the world's biggest wind tunnel in California, USA.

19 The ever-changing positions of Earth and other objects in space mean there is a limited 'launch window' for each mission. This is when Earth is in the best position for a craft to reach its target in the shortest time. If the launch window is missed, the distances may become too massive.

20 In space, repairs are difficult or impossible. Exploring craft must be incredibly reliable, with tested and proven technology. Each piece of equipment needs a back-up, and even if this fails, it should not affect other parts.

▼ The *New Horizons* spacecraft was assembled and checked in perfectly clean, dust-free conditions before being launched to Pluto in 2006.

The robot submarine *Endurance*, which may one day explore oceans on distant planets or moons, has been tested in frozen lakes in Antarctica and near-boiling pools in New Zealand.

21 A spacecraft must be able to cope with the conditions in space and on other worlds. It is incredibly cold in space, but planets such as Venus are hotter than boiling water. Other planets have hazards such as clouds made of tiny drops of acid.

▶ The spacecraft *Galileo* was tested in ultra-bright light of the same level that it would receive as it flew nearer the Sun in 1990 on its way to Jupiter.

22 A test version of the spacecraft is tried on Earth. If successful, the real craft is built in strict conditions. One loose screw or speck of dust could cause disaster. There's no second chance once the mission begins.

Blast-off!

23 A spacecraft is blasted into space by its launch vehicle, or rocket. The rocket is the only machine powerful enough to reach 'escape velocity' – the speed needed to break free from the pull of Earth's gravity. The spacecraft is usually folded up in the nose cone of the rocket.

24 Different sizes of rockets are used for different sizes of spacecraft. One of the heaviest was the *Cassini-Huygens* mission to Saturn. At its launch in 1997, with all its fuel and equipment on board, it weighed 5.6 tonnes – almost as much as a school bus. It needed a huge *Titan IV* rocket launcher to power it into space.

25 Spacecraft and other objects carried by the rocket are called the 'payload'. Most rockets take their payload into orbit around the Earth. The nose cone opens to release the craft stored inside. Parts of it unfold, such as the solar panels that turn sunlight into electricity.

Launch point

Escape velocity

Orbit bound by Earth's gravity

◄ Launch vehicles must quickly reach escape velocity – 11,200 metres per second – to shrug off Earth's gravitational pull.

SECOND STAGE (S-II)
The middle section of the launcher had five J-2 rocket engines. It was 25 metres tall, and like the first stage, was 10 metres wide.

FIRST STAGE (S-IC)
The bottom part of *Saturn V* was 42 metres tall. The F-1 rocket engines propelled the entire launch vehicle for the first 60 kilomentres.

J-2 rocket engines

F-1 rocket engines

▲ The biggest launchers were the three-stage *Saturn V* rockets used to launch the Apollo missions. Each stage fell away after using up its fuel.

▶ Europe's *Ariane 5* has one main rocket engine and two boosters. These boosters burn for the first 129 seconds, then detach.

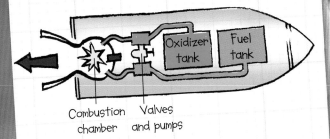

Combustion chamber   Valves and pumps

Oxidizer tank   Fuel tank

▲ Liquid-fuel rocket engines have a tank of liquid fuel and a tank of liquid oxygen or an oxygen-rich chemical. When the two mix together and ignite, they burn and create thrust.

THIRD STAGE (S-IVB)
The third stage was 17.8 metres tall and 6.6 metres wide. It had one J-2 engine (like those in the second stage).

Launch escape tower

Command Module

Service Module

Lunar Module

J-2 rocket engine

26 Craft are tested while in orbit around the Earth, to check the engines, radio communications, cameras and other parts are working. If there is a problem, a robot repair mission or some astronauts may be sent up. If everything is in working order, the craft can boost away from Earth to begin its long journey.

MAKE A ROCKET
You will need:
sheet of card   cardboard tube   sticky tape   scissors

Use the tube for the main body of the rocket. Make a cone shape with some of the card and stick it to one end. In a safe place, 'launch' the rocket by throwing it up at an angle. It should tumble out of control. Add fins by sticking four large, card triangles to the base. Now it should fly much straighter.

In deep space

27 Most spacecraft travel for months, even years, to their destinations. The fastest journey to Mars took just over six months, by *Mars Express* in 2003. *Pioneer 10* took 11 years to reach Neptune in 1983.

◀ *Mars Express* cruised at a speed of 10,800 kilometres an hour on its way to Mars.

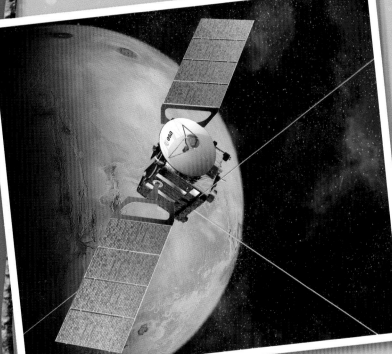

28 Guiding the craft on its course is vital. A tiny error could mean that it misses its distant target by millions of kilometres. Mission controllers on Earth regularly check the craft's position with radio signals using the Deep Space Network (DSN). The DSN is made up of three huge radio dishes located in California, USA, Madrid in Spain, and Canberra, Australia.

▼ This ion thruster is being tested in a vacuum chamber. The blue glow is the beam of charged atoms being thrown out of the engine.

29 Spacecraft only need small engines because there is no air in space to slow them down. Depending on the length of the journey, different kinds of engines and fuels are used. The ion thruster uses magnetism made by electricity. This hurls tiny particles, called ions, backwards, which pushes the craft forwards.

◄ Bowl-shaped antennae (aerials), like *New Horizons'*, exchange radio signals to and from Earth.

30 Craft often pass other planets or moons on their journeys. Like Earth, these objects all have a gravitational pull, and this could send a craft off course. However, a planet's gravity may be used to propel the craft in a new direction to save fuel. This is known as a gravity assist flyby or 'slingshot'.

Saturn

Venus

Earth

Jupiter

▲ *Cassini-Huygens'* journey to Saturn involved four gravity-assists. The main stages were: launch to first Venus flyby (orange), second Venus flyby (blue), and Earth flyby, past Jupiter to Saturn (purple).

KEY

1 October 1997 Launch from Earth

2 April 1998 First Venus flyby

3 December 1998 Engine fires for 90 minutes to return to Venus

4 June 1999 Second Venus flyby

5 August 1999 Earth-Moon flyby

6 December 2000 Jupiter flyby

7 July 2004 Arrives in orbit around Saturn

Goldstone, California, USA

Madrid, Spain

Canberra, Australia

◄ ▼ The three Deep Space Network sites are equally spaced around Earth, with 120 degrees between them, making a 360-degree circle.

31 For long periods, much of a craft's equipment shuts down to save electricity. It's like an animal hibernating in winter or a mobile phone on stand-by. When the craft 'hibernates' only a few vital systems stay active, such as navigation.

► The Deep Space Network's radio dish at Goldstone near Barstow, California, is 70 metres across.

32 As the spacecraft approaches its target, its systems power up and it 'comes to life'. Controllers on Earth test the craft's radio communications and other equipment. At such enormous distances, radio signals can take minutes, even hours, to make the journey.

33 Among the most important devices onboard a craft are cameras. Some work like telescopes to take a close-up or magnified view of a small area. Others are wide-angle cameras, which capture a much greater area without magnifying.

34 Other kinds of camera can 'see' types of waves that are invisible to the human eye. These include infrared or heat rays, ultraviolet rays, radio waves and X-rays. These rays and waves provide information about the target world, such as how hot or cold it is.

▼ *Mars Reconnaissance Orbiter's* photograph of the 730-metre-wide Victoria Crater was captured by its high-resolution camera and shows amazing detail.

The Mars Climate Sounder records the temperature, moisture and dust in the Martian atmosphere

The high-resolution camera captures close-up, detailed photographs of the surface

QUIZ

Spacecraft have many devices, but rarely microphones to detect sound. Why?

A. The chance of meeting aliens who can shout loudly is very small.

B. Sound waves do not travel through the vacuum of space.

C. It's too difficult to change sound waves into radio signals.

Answer: B

Antenna

35 Magnetometers detect magnetic fields, which exist naturally around some planets, including Earth. Gravitometers measure the target object's pull of gravity. This is especially important in the final stage of the journey – the landing. Some spacecraft also have space dust collectors.

Solar panel

◄ *Mars Reconnaissance Orbiter*, launched in 2005, carries a telescopic camera, wide-angle cameras, sensors for infrared and ultraviolet light and a radar that 'sees' below the surface.

The spectrometer identifies different substances on the surface by measuring how much light is reflected

36 The information from the cameras and sensors is turned into radio signal codes and beamed back to Earth. To send and receive these signals, the craft has one or more dish-shaped antennae. These must be in the correct position to communicate with the dishes located on Earth.

The sub-surface radar can see up to one kilometre below the planet's surface

Flyby, bye-bye

37 On a flyby mission, a spacecraft comes close to its target. It does not go into orbit around it or land – it flies onwards and away into deep space. Some flybys are part of longer missions to even more distant destinations. In these cases the flyby may also involve gravity assist.

LAUNCH
FROM EARTH
20 August, 1977

JUPITER

38 A flyby craft may pass its target several times on a long, lop-sided path, before leaving again. Each pass gives a different view of the target object. The craft's cameras, sensors and other equipment switch on to take pictures and record measurements, then turn off again as it flies away.

Flyby on 9 July, 1979

39 The ultimate flyby craft was *Voyager 2*. It made a 'Grand Tour' of the four outermost planets, which are only suitably aligned every 175 years. *Voyager 2* blasted off in 1977 and flew past Jupiter in 1979, Saturn in 1981, Uranus in 1986 and Neptune in 1989. This craft is still sending back information from a distance twice as far as Pluto is from Earth.

I DON'T BELIEVE IT!
When *Pioneer 11* zoomed to within 43,000 kilometres of Jupiter in 1974, it made the fastest-ever flyby at 50 kilometres per second.

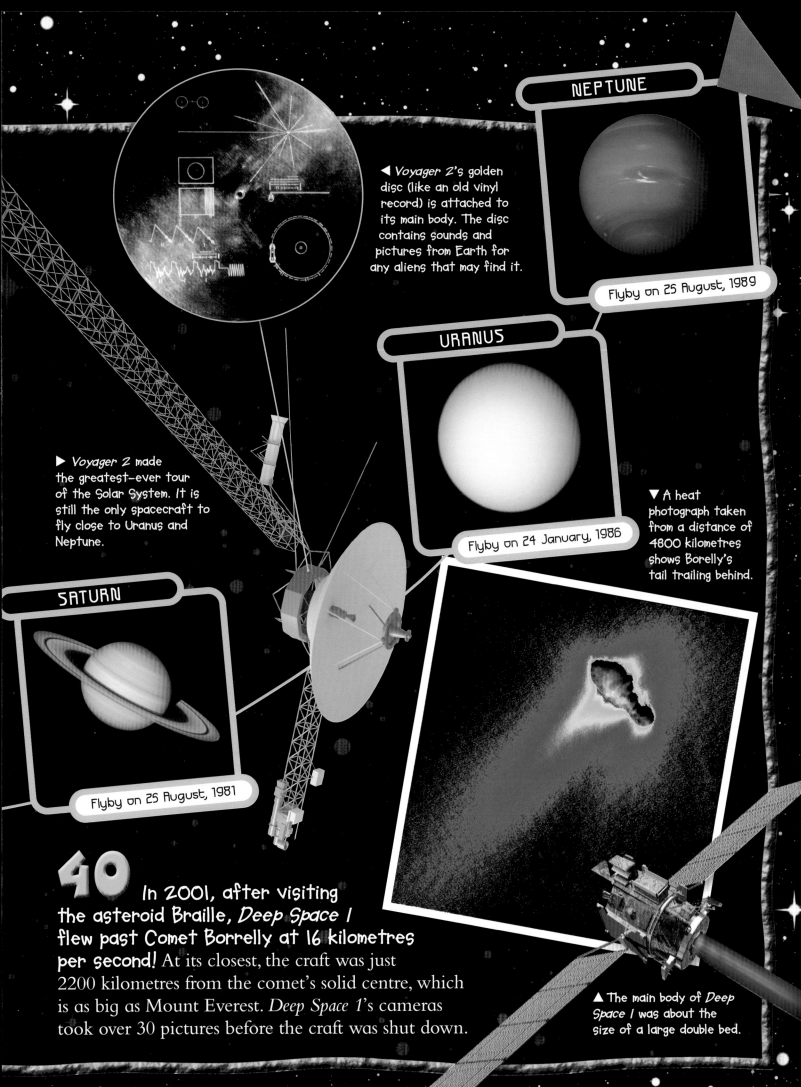

◀ *Voyager 2's* golden disc (like an old vinyl record) is attached to its main body. The disc contains sounds and pictures from Earth for any aliens that may find it.

NEPTUNE

Flyby on 25 August, 1989

URANUS

Flyby on 24 January, 1986

▶ *Voyager 2* made the greatest-ever tour of the Solar System. It is still the only spacecraft to fly close to Uranus and Neptune.

▼ A heat photograph taken from a distance of 4800 kilometres shows Borelly's tail trailing behind.

SATURN

Flyby on 25 August, 1981

40 In 2001, after visiting the asteroid Braille, *Deep Space 1* flew past Comet Borrelly at 16 kilometres per second! At its closest, the craft was just 2200 kilometres from the comet's solid centre, which is as big as Mount Everest. *Deep Space 1*'s cameras took over 30 pictures before the craft was shut down.

▲ The main body of *Deep Space 1* was about the size of a large double bed.

Into orbit

41 On many exploring missions the craft is designed to go into orbit around its target world. Craft that do this are called orbiters, and they provide a much longer, closer look than a flyby mission.

▶ There are several different types of orbit that craft can make around their targets. Here, they are shown around Earth.

A polar orbit passes over the North and South Poles

An equatorial orbit goes around the middle (Equator)

Most orbits are elliptical, with low and high points

42 One of the most elliptical orbits was made by *Mars Global Surveyor*. At its closest, it passed Mars at a distance of 171 kilometres, twice in each orbit. The craft's furthest distance away was more than ten times greater.

◀ In 2006, two twin STEREO-craft went into orbit around the Sun. With one in front and one behind Earth, the craft made the first 3D observations of the Sun.

Antenna

ORBITER
You will need:
sock   tennis ball   string (one metre long)
Put the ball in the sock and tie up the top with the string. Go outside. Holding the string half way along its length, whirl the sock above your head so that it 'orbits' you. Gradually lengthen the string – does the 'orbit' take longer?

During its orbits of Saturn, Cassini passed Dione, Saturn's 15th largest moon. Saturn can be seen in the distance.

43 The *Cassini* orbiter, part of the *Cassini–Huygens* mission, has been through many changes of orbit around Saturn. Some went close to the main planet and some passed near to its rings. Other orbits took it past Saturn's largest moon, Titan, and its smaller moons, including Enceladus, Iapetus and Mimas.

44 A spacecraft's radar checks its average height above the surface. Radio or microwave signals beam down to the surface and bounce back. The time this takes tells the craft how far away it is. More detailed radar measurements map the surface far below.

Camera

45 A spectrometer analyzes different colours in light waves. Different chemical substances give off or reflect certain colours of light better than others. By reading this, the spectrometer can work out what substances are present in a planet's atmosphere or on its surface.

▶ *Mars Global Surveyor's* average orbital height was 378 kilometres. It mapped the entire Martian surface.

Solar panel

46 The orbiter continually checks and adjusts its height and position. It does this using tiny puffs of gas from its thrusters, which stops the craft losing speed and crashing into the surface.

Landers and impactors

47 Some missions have landers that touch down onto the surface of their target world. Part of the spacecraft may detach and land while the other part stays in orbit, or the whole spacecraft may land.

① Spacecraft in orbit

② Landing module separates from orbiter

③ First parachute opened, then detached

▶ The later landers of the Russian *Venera* program (1961–1983) used parachutes to slow down in the thick, hot, cloudy atmosphere of Venus.

48 The journey down can be hazardous. If the planet has an atmosphere (layer of gas around it) there may be strong winds that could blow the lander off course. If the atmosphere is thick, there may be huge pressure pushing on the craft.

④ Main parachutes opened at a height of 50 kilometres above the surface

49 If there is an atmosphere, the lander may use parachutes, or inflate its own balloons or air bags, to slow its speed. On the *Cassini-Huygens* mission, the *Huygens* lander used two parachutes as it descended for touchdown on Saturn's moon, Titan.

⑤ Ring-shaped shock absorber filled with compressed gas lessened the impact at touchdown

50 If there is no atmosphere, retro-thrusters are used to slow the craft down. These puff gases in the direction of travel. Most landers have a strong, bouncy casing for protection as they hit the surface, or long, springy legs to reduce the impact.

▲ A photograph taken by *Deep Impact* 67 seconds after its impactor crashed into Comet Tempel 1, shows material being thrown out.

51 **After touchdown, the lander's solar panels and other parts fold out.** Its equipment and systems switch on, and it tests its radio communications with the orbiter and sometimes directly with Earth.

▲ This image shows how *Beagle 2*'s solar panels were designed to fold out. However contact with the lander was lost soon after it detached from its orbiter in 2003.

Impactor

52 **Some craft are designed to smash into their target, and these are called impactors.** The crash is observed by the orbiter and may also be watched by controllers on Earth. The dust, rocks and gases given off by an impact provide valuable information about the target object.

Camera

▶ In 2005, *Deep Impact* released its impactor, watched it strike Comet Tempel 1 and studied the resulting crater.

◀ *Mars Pathfinder* lander being tested on Earth. It used a parachute, retro-thrusters and multi-bubble airbags to land on Mars.

Robotic rovers

53 After touchdown, some landers release small, robotic vehicles called rovers. They have wheels and motors so they can move around on the surface to explore. So far rovers have explored on the Moon and Mars.

Antennae

Laser reflector

Solar panels

Cameras

Wheels

▶ In the 1970s, Russia sent two rovers, *Lunokhod 1* and *2*, to the Moon. Each was the size of a large bathtub, weighed almost one tonne and had eight wheels driven by electric motors.

QUIZ

How were the Mars rovers *Spirit* and *Opportunity* named?

1. Words chosen at random.
2. By a group of space experts.
3. By a 9-year-old girl, who won a competition.

Answer:
3. Siberian-born American schoolgirl Sofi Collis won the 2003 'Name the Rovers' competition.

54 Modern rovers are mostly robotic – self-controlled using onboard computers. This is because of the time delay of radio signals. Even when Earth and Mars are at their closest distance to each other, radio signals take over three minutes to travel one way. If a rover was driven by remote control from Earth, it could have fallen off a cliff long before its onboard cameras relayed images of this.

55
Rovers are designed and tested to survive the conditions on their target world. Scientists know about these conditions from information collected from observations on Earth, and from previous missions. Test rovers are driven on extreme landscapes on Earth to make sure they can handle tricky terrain.

▲ A test version of a new rover destined for Mars, here being tested on the slippery rocks of a beach in Wales, Uk.

56
The *Spirit* and *Opportunity* rovers landed on Mars in 2004. They are equipped with cameras that allow them to navigate around obstacles. Heat-sensitive cameras detect levels of heat soaked up by rocks, giving clues to what the rocks are made of. On-board microscopes and magnets gather and study dust particles containing iron.

Navcam

Antenna

Main antenna

Solar panels

▶ Twin rovers *Spirit* and *Opportunity* are each about the size of an office desk.

Mobile arm carries five gadgets including a camera, rock grinder and magnets

Each wheel has an electric motor

57
A rover for Venus is planned, but its surface temperature is over 400°C. Plastics and some metals would melt there. A Venus rover would have to be made out of metals such as titanium, which have high melting points. Its inner workings would need to be continually cooled.

▶ In the late 1970s the USA's two Viking landers photographed their robotic sampler arms digging into Mars' surface.

Solar panel

58 **Some landers and rovers have robot arms that extend from the main body.** These scoop or drill into the surface to collect samples, which are then tested in the craft's onboard science laboratory. Samples are tested for chemical reactions, such as bubbling or changing colour.

Robotic arm with scoop and camera

Spheres of minerals containing iron, known as 'blueberries'

Circular area ground by tool is 4.5 centimetres across

59 **Most rovers have six wheels.** This design allows them to move quickly around sharp corners, without tipping over. Each wheel has an electric motor, powered by onboard batteries that are charged by the solar panels. If the batteries run down, the rover 'sleeps' until light from the Sun recharges them.

◀ Mars rovers *Spirit* and *Opportunity* are both equipped with a rock-grinding tool. They use it to grind into rocks and gather dust samples.

60 The *Phoenix* Mars lander had several devices on its robotic arm to measure features of Martian soil. It measured how easily it carried (conducted) heat and electricity, and if it contained any liquids. *Phoenix* also had microscopes for an ultra-close view of the surface samples.

Meteorological (weather) station

Gas analyzers

Mini science laboratory

Solar panel

61 Most landers and rovers have mini weather stations. Sensors measure temperatures and pressures through the day and night and record the Sun's brightness. They also take samples of gases if there is an atmosphere, and record weather, such as wind and dust storms.

◀ The *Phoenix* Mars lander of 2008 had a robotic arm, on the left, and a small weather station.

62 The orbiting craft acts as a relay station to receive signals from its lander and send them on to Earth. A lander can in turn be a relay station for a rover. A rover has a small radio set to communicate with the lander and the lander has a slightly larger one to communicate with the orbiter. The orbiter has the biggest radio set to communicate with Earth.

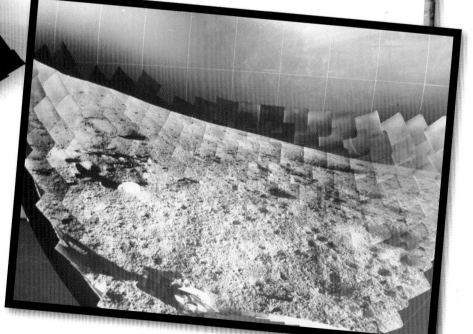

▲ In the 1960s five US Surveyor landers sent back separate close-up photographs of the Moon's surface. These were joined together to make larger scenes.

Exploring Mars

JUL 1965 *Mariner 4* flew past Mars and took the first close-up photos of another planet

NOV 1971 *Mariner 9* entered orbit around Mars — the first craft to orbit another planet

63 Mars is the nearest planet to Earth and the most explored. In the 1870s, astronomers thought they could see canals of water on Mars' surface, thought to be built by aliens. But with better telescopes, these 'canals' were found to be simply a trick of the light.

▼ This timeline shows some of the most notable missions in the exploration of Mars.

DEC 1971 *Mars 3*'s lander was the first to touch down safely on Mars, but contact was lost after 20 seconds

64 Since the 1960s more than 40 missions have set off to Mars. About two-thirds of them failed at launch or on the way. One-quarter have failed at or near Mars, leading some people to believe that Martians were attacking and destroying the craft.

JUL/SEP 1976 *Viking 1* and *2* were the first successful landers on the surface of Mars

JUL 1997 *Mars Pathfinder* landed and released *Sojourner*, the first rover, on another planet

◀ *Mars Odyssey* (2001) produced this image of Mars' south pole. The Martian polar ice caps are made of frozen water and 'dry ice' — solid (frozen) carbon dioxide.

65 In 1976, two US Viking landers carried out research on Mars. They took many photographs, made detailed maps and tested the atmosphere, rocks and soil, but they found no definite signs of life. In 2008, the US *Phoenix* lander discovered water frozen as ice, and many minerals and chemicals in the soil.

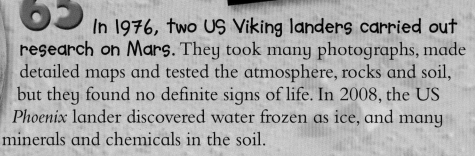

66 The *Spirit* and *Opportunity* rovers have made an amazing series of explorations and discoveries. They have found evidence that there was once water on Mars, and that it is possibly still there underground. In 2009 *Spirit* got stuck in soft soil but *Opportunity* is still moving, although very slowly.

MAY 2008 *Phoenix* lander touched down. It was the first craft to land in Mars' polar area

DEC 2003 In orbit, *Mars Express* released its lander, *Beagle 2*, but communications to it were lost

SEP 1997 *Mars Global Surveyor* went into orbit and began detailed, large-scale mapping of the surface

MAR 2006 *Mars Reconnaissance Orbiter* arrived, making a record six working craft in orbit or on the surface of Mars

67 The *Mars Science Laboratory* rover, planned for 2011, has a drill, scoop arm and several packages of experiments. It is the biggest-ever rover at almost one tonne in weight. Its aim is to find out if there is, or ever has been, any life on Mars.

JAN 2004 *Mars Exploration Rovers Spirit* and *Opportunity* arrived on the surface, ready to explore

◄ *Mars Science Laboratory* is about the size of a Mini car and has a top speed of 2.5 centimetres per second.

68 **All spacecraft have a mission control centre on Earth.** Expert teams monitor a craft's systems, including radio communications, and the data a craft collects from its cameras and instruments.

▲ Mission controllers at NASA's Jet Propulsion Laboratory in California, USA, celebrate as the first images from rover *Opportunity* reach Earth.

69 **Missions often run into problems.** Controllers must work out how to keep a mission going when faults occur. If power supplies fail, the teams may have to decide to switch off some equipment so that others can continue working.

70 **Sample return missions bring items from space back to Earth.** In 2004, the *Genesis* craft dropped off its return container. It was supposed to parachute down to Earth's surface, but it crash-landed in Utah, USA. Luckily, some of its samples of solar wind survived for study.

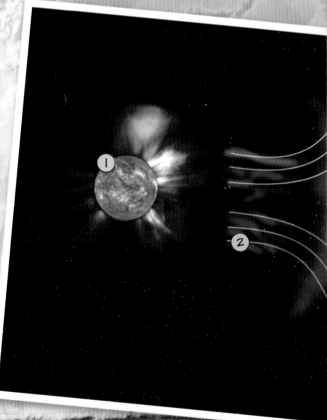

71 Gases, dust, rocks and other items are brought back to Earth to be studied. In the early 1970s the six manned Apollo missions brought a total of 381.7 kilograms of Moon material back to Earth.

▲ This piece of basalt Moon rock, brought back by *Apollo 15*, is being studied by *Apollo 17* astronaut and geologist (rock expert) Jack Schmitt.

72 Samples returned from space must not be contaminated with material from Earth. Keeping samples clean allows scientists to find out what they contain, and stops any dangerous substances being released on Earth. Spacecraft are ultra-clean at launch to prevent them spreading chemicals or germs from Earth to other worlds.

▼ *Genesis* collected high-energy particles from the Sun's solar wind, which distorts Earth's magnetic field.

► This sample of Moon rock collected during the *Apollo 11* misison is housed inside a securely fastened, airtight container.

KEY
1. Sun
2. Solar wind
3. Bow shock (where the solar wind meets Earth's magnetic field)
4. Earth's magnetic field
5. Earth

◄ This photograph taken by *SOHO* uses a disc with a hole to block out some of the Sun's glare. This reveals vast streaming clouds of superheated matter called plasma.

Corona

Coronal mass ejection (CME) of superheated plasma

73 Missions to the Sun encounter enormous heat. In the 1970s the US–German craft *Helios 2* flew to within 44 million kilometres of the Sun. From 1990, the *Ulysses* probe travelled on a huge orbit, passing near the Sun and as far out as Jupiter.

74 In 1996, the *SOHO* satellite began studying the Sun from near Earth. Since then, it has found many new comets. In 2015, *Solar Probe Plus* will orbit to within six million kilometres of the Sun, with a shield-like 'sunshade' of heat-resistant, carbon-composite material for protection.

1c
HELIOS MISSION
GRENADA

◄ The Helios mission was featured on stamps worldwide.

76 Mercury, the nearest planet to the Sun, has been visited by two spacecraft, *Mariner 10* in 1974, and *Messenger* in 2004. *Messenger* made flybys in 2008 and 2009 and is due in orbit in 2011. These craft measured Mercury's surface temperature at 420°C – twice as hot as a home oven.

▲ *Messenger* had a 'sunshade' made out of a ceramic–composite material to protect it from the Sun's heat.

77 More than 20 craft have visited Venus, the second planet from the Sun. Its atmosphere of thick clouds, extreme pressures, temperatures over 450°C and acid chemicals, pose huge challenges for exploring craft.

75 Missions to Venus include Russia's Venera series (1961 to 1984), US Mariner probes (1962 to 1973) and *Pioneer Venus* (1978). From 1990 to 1994, *Magellan* used a radar to map the surface in amazing detail. In 2006, Europe's *Venus Express* began more mapping. Its instruments also studied Venus' extreme global warming.

◄ Studying Venus' atmosphere may help us understand similar climate processes happening on Earth.

Antenna

Solar panel

Positioning thrusters

Main rocket engine

Gold coating helps to keep out the Sun's heat

▲ *Venus Express* orbits as low as 250 kilometres above the poles of Venus.

I DON'T BELIEVE IT!
The fastest spacecraft, and the fastest man–made object ever, was *Helios 2*. It neared the Sun at 67 kilometres per second!

Asteroids near and far

78 Asteroids orbit the Sun but are far smaller than planets, so even finding them is a challenge. Most large asteroids are in the main asteroid belt between Mars and Jupiter. Much closer to us are near-Earth Asteroids (NEAs), and more than 20 have been explored in detail by flyby craft, orbiters and landers.

Mars

79 Orbiting and landing on asteroids is very difficult. Many asteroids are oddly shaped, and they roll and tumble as they move through space. A craft may only discover this as it gets close.

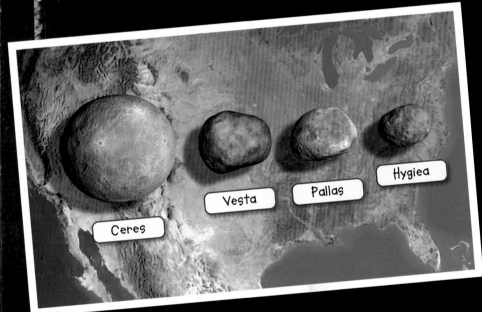

Ceres
Vesta
Pallas
Hygiea

◀ Dwarf planet Ceres and the three largest asteroids in our Solar System, seen against North America for scale. Vesta, the biggest asteroid, is about 530 kilometres across.

80 In 1996, the probe NEAR-Shoemaker launched towards NEA Eros. On the way it flew past asteroid Mathilde in the main belt. Then in 2000 it orbited 34-kilometre-long Eros, before landing. The probe discoverd that the asteroid was peanut-shaped, and also gathered information about Eros' rocks, magnetism and movement. In 2008, spacecraft *Rosetta* passed main belt asteroid Steins, and asteroid Lutetia in 2010.

Jupiter

▲ In the main belt there are some dense 'asteroid swarms'. But most larger asteroids are tens of thousands of kilometres apart.

81 In 2010 Japan's *Hayabusa* brought back samples of asteroid Itokawa after touching down on its surface in 2005. This information has helped our understanding of asteroids as 'leftovers' from the formation of the Solar System 4600 million years ago.

82 *Dawn* was launched in 2007, to explore Vesta – the biggest asteroid – in 2011 and the dwarf planet Ceres in 2015. Vesta may be rocky, while Ceres is thought to be icier, with various chemicals frozen as solids. *Dawn* aims find out for sure.

▲ The *Dawn* mission badge shows its two main targets.

▶ *Hayabusa* was designed to gather samples of the asteroid Itokawa by firing a metal pellet towards the surface. It could then collect the dust thrown up by the impact.

Comet mysteries

83 Comets travel to and from the edges of the Solar System and beyond as they orbit the Sun. Unlike long-period comets, which may take thousands of years to orbit, short-period comets orbit every 200 years or less and so can be explored.

▶ The Oort cloud surrounds the Solar System and is made up of icy objects. It may be the source of some Sun-orbiting comets.

Sun

Kuiper belt

▶ The Kuiper belt lies beyond Neptune's orbit and is about twice the size of the Solar System. It consists of lots of comet-like objects.

Neptune

84 Like asteroids, comets are difficult to find. Comets warm up and glow only as they near the Sun. Their tails are millions of kilometres long, but consist only of faint gases and dust. The centre, or nucleus, of a comet may give off powerful jets of dust and gases that could blow a craft off course.

▶ A typical comet is mostly dust and ice. It has a glowing area, or coma, around it, and a long tail that points away from the Sun.

Solid rock core

Nucleus is often only a few kilometres across

Jets of gas and dust escape as ice melts

Glowing cloud, or coma, around nucleus is illuminated by sunlight

Dust and ice surrounds core

Comet dust particles

85

The famous Halley's Comet last appeared in 1986.
Several exploring craft, known as the 'Halley Armada', went to visit it. This included Europe's *Giotto* probe, which flew to within 600 kilometres of the comet's nucleus. There were also two Russian-French Vega probes, and *Sakigake* and *Suisei* from Japan.

▲ Under the microscope, a piece of *Stardust*'s aerogel (half the size of this 'o') is revealed to have minute dust particles embedded within it.

▶ *Stardust* collected comet dust using a very lightweight foam, called aerogel, in a collector shaped like a tennis bat. The collector folded into the craft's bowl-like capsule for return to Earth.

86

In 2008, the *Stardust* probe returned a capsule of dust collected from the comet Wild 2. In 2005, *Deep Impact* visited Comet Tempel 1 and released an impactor to crash into its nucleus and study the dust and gases given off. These craft increase our knowledge of comets as frozen balls of icy chemicals, rock and dust.

STARDUST APPROACHING COMET WILD 2

Glowing dust tail
illuminated by sunlight

Ion (gas) tail
appears bluish

SAMPLE CAPSULE RETURNS TO EARTH

Gas giants

I DON'T BELIEVE IT!
A craft entering Neptune's atmosphere would be hit by the fastest winds in the Solar System – ten times stronger than a hurricane on Earth!

87 The four furthest planets from Earth – Jupiter, Saturn, Uranus and Neptune – are 'gas giants'. These are large planets composed mainly of gases. It takes at least two years to reach Jupiter by the most direct route. But craft usually take longer because they use gravity assist.

▼ *Galileo* orbited Jupiter for more than seven years. It released an atmosphere probe to study the gases that make up almost the whole planet.

88 There have been seven flybys of Jupiter and each one discovered more of the planet's moons. The two US Voyager missions, launched in 1977, discovered that Jupiter has rings like Saturn. US spacecraft *Galileo* arrived in orbit around Jupiter in 1995 and released a probe into the planet's atmosphere.

▲ *Huygens'* pictures from the surface of Titan, Saturn's largest moon, show lumps of ice and a haze of deadly methane gas.

89

The ringed planet Saturn had flybys by *Pioneer 11* (1979) and *Voyagers 1* and *2* (1980–1981). In 2004 the huge *Cassini-Huygens* craft arrived after a seven-year journey. The orbiter *Cassini* is still taking spectacular photographs of the planet, its rings and its moons.

▼ The *Huygens* lander separated from *Cassini* and headed for Titan. It sent back more than 750 images from the surface.

TITAN

A heat shield prevented burn–up on entry

Parachutes slowed the lander's descent

Huygens lands on Titan

90

The only exploring craft to have visited Uranus and Neptune is *Voyager 2*. During its flyby of Uranus in 1986, *Voyager 2* discovered ten new moons and two new rings. In 1989, the craft passed the outermost planet, Neptune, and discovered six new moons and four new rings.

▼ The four gas giants have many moons — some large, and some very small. This list includes the five largest moons for each (not to scale).

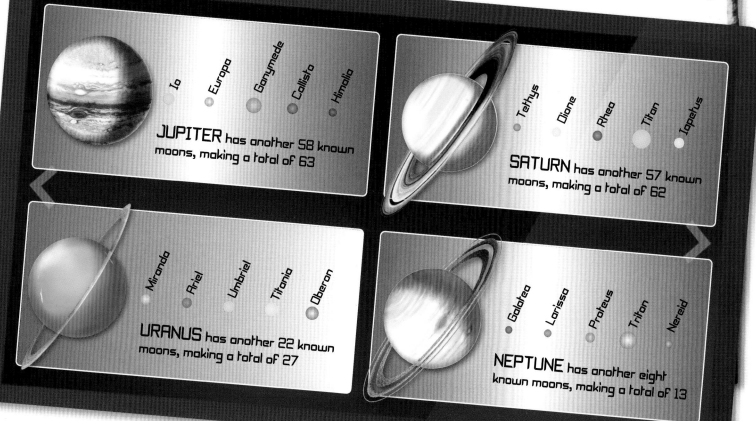

Io Europa Ganymede Callisto Himalia

JUPITER has another 58 known moons, making a total of 63

Tethys Dione Rhea Titan Iapetus

SATURN has another 57 known moons, making a total of 62

Miranda Ariel Umbriel Titania Oberon

URANUS has another 22 known moons, making a total of 27

Galatea Larissa Proteus Triton Nereid

NEPTUNE has another eight known moons, making a total of 13

Into the future

91 Sending craft to the edges of the Solar System takes many years. US spacecraft *New Horizons* was launched in 2006, and is now heading for dwarf planet Pluto. The craft is due to reach Pluto in 2015 and may continue into the Kuiper Belt, the home of comets and more dwarf planets.

92 *New Horizons'* immense nine-year journey was complicated to plan. It includes a flyby of tiny asteroid 132534 APL, then a swing around Jupiter for gravity assist and a speed boost. Flybys of Jupiter's moons are also planned, before the long cruise to tiny Pluto. Without Jupiter's gravity assist, the trip would be five years longer.

◀ *New Horizons'* dish-shaped antenna is as big as a double bed. The grey, finned cylinder to the left is a tiny nuclear generator for electricity — solar panels are useless so far away from the Sun.

93 Several major explorations are planned for the coming years. The *ExoMars* mission consists of a lander and a rover, due to launch in 2016 and 2018. They will look for signs of life on Mars, using a 2-metre-deep drill. The *BepiColombo* mission aims to orbit Mercury and measure the Sun's power.

◄ The *BepiColombo* mission is planned for launch in 2014. The six-year trip will take the craft past the Moon, Earth and Venus before reaching Mercury — the closest planet to the Sun.

Drill

▲ The drill on *ExoMars* rover will pass soil samples to the mini laboratory on board for analysis.

94 What happens to exploring spacecraft? Some are deliberately crashed into other worlds, so that the impact can be observed by other spacecraft or from Earth. Others burn up as they enter the atmosphere of a planet or large moon.

95 Many exploring spacecraft are still travelling in space, and will be for thousands of years. As they run out of power they become silent, either sitting on their target worlds or drifting though empty space — unless they crash into an object. The most distant craft is *Voyager 1*, launched in 1977. It is now more than 17 billion kilometres from Earth, and is still being tracked.

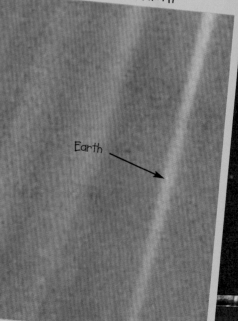

FAR-AWAY EARTH

Earth

► The 'Pale Blue Dot' photograph captured in 1990 by *Voyager 1*, was taken from six billion kilometres away. Earth is the tiny speck.

Space magic and myth

96 Exploring space has long been a favourite subject for story-telling. Even before rockets, there were theories about space travel and aliens. One of the first was *War of the Worlds*, written in 1898 by H G Wells.

▲ H G Wells' original story is brought to life in the 1953 movie *War of the Worlds*, in which martians invade Earth and destroy city after city. Humans can't stop them, but instead, germs eventually wipe out the alien invaders.

◄ The mission statement of *Star Trek*'s starship *Enterprise* was: 'To explore strange new worlds, to seek out new life and new civilizations, to boldly go where no one has gone before.'

97 In the 1950s, as humans began to explore space, tales of sightings of 'flying saucers' and UFOs (Unidentified Flying Objects) soared. Some of these may be explained by secret aircraft or spacecraft being tested by governments. A few people claimed that aliens visited Earth and left signs, such as strange patterns in fields called crop circles.

98 The *Star Wars* (1977–2005) and *Alien* movies (1979–2007) are all about adventures in space. This genre grew in popularity at the same time that space exploration was becoming a reality. The *Star Trek* movies (1979 onwards) had several spin-off television series, including *Voyager* and *Deep Space Nine*.

99 In the future, scientists may discover a form of ultra-fast travel involving black holes and wormholes (tunnels through space and time). This could allow humans to travel to distant galaxies to look for other 'Goldilocks' planets similar to Earth. Like the third bowl of porridge in the nursery story, the conditions on a Goldilocks planet are not too hot and not too cold, but 'just right' for life to exist. As yet, no others have been discovered.

QUIZ

1. What was the name of the story written by H G Wells about an alien invasion of Earth?
2. What does UFO stand for?
3. What is a 'Goldilocks' planet?

Answers:
1. *War of the Worlds*
2. Unidentified Flying Object
3. A planet that has the perfect conditions for life to exist – not too hot, not too cold, but 'just right'.

100 Space scientists have suggested new kinds of rockets and thrusters for faster space travel. These could reduce the journey time to the next-nearest star, Proxima Centauri, to about 100 years. But one day we may be beaten to it – aliens from a distant galaxy could be exploring space right now and discover us first!

N33955

▼ Virgin Galactic will soon be offering space travel to the general public. A ticket for a flight on *SpaceShipTwo* (below) will cost $200,000!

Index

Entries in **bold** refer to main subject entries; entries in *italics* refer to illustrations.